MINNESOTA DRAMA EDITIONS NO. 3
Edited by Tyrone Guthrie

FIVE EVENINGS

by ALEKSANDR VOLODIN

translated and adapted by
ARIADNE NICOLAEFF

Minneapolis
UNIVERSITY OF MINNESOTA PRESS IN ASSOCIATION
WITH THE MINNESOTA THEATRE COMPANY

PUBLISHED IN GREAT BRITAIN, INDIA, AND PAKISTAN BY THE
OXFORD UNIVERSITY PRESS, LONDON, BOMBAY, AND KARACHI,
AND IN CANADA BY THE COPP CLARK PUBLISHING CO.
LIMITED, TORONTO

CONTENTS

===

FIVE EVENINGS

ABOUT THE PLAYWRIGHT

BY ARIADNE NICOLAEFF

By the late nineteen-fifties Aleksandr Volodin had established himself as an important new voice in the Soviet theatre. Along with Viktor Rozov and Samuil Alyoshin, who came to prominence about the same time, he represents a "new wave" of Soviet dramatists, who appear to be primarily interested in personal relationships and values within a framework that is social rather than specifically socialist or communist. The interests of Volodin and his contemporaries are similar to those of a group of Soviet playwrights of the early nineteen-thirties, of whom Vasily Shkvarkin was outstanding.

Born on February 10, 1919, Aleksandr Moiseyevich Volodin (pseudonym for Lifshitz) graduated from the Scenario faculty of the National Institute of Cinematography in 1949. He began his literary career in 1954. In 1957 his early play

The Factory Kid became the center of violent controversy in the Soviet press.

Stalinist critics attacked *The Factory Kid* because its villain was a Party official, the head of the Young Communist League organization in a factory, and its heroine was a plain-spoken, fun-loving girl without strong political interests. The play's defenders were vociferous in insisting that Volodin was dramatizing the evils of bureaucracy, not of the Party or state as such. While the critical controversy raged, *The Factory Kid* was being enthusiastically received by large audiences.

Five Evenings was first published in the monthly theatre journal *Teatr* in 1958 and it was produced at the Bolshoi Theatre of Drama in 1959. A later play, *Going Out and Staying In*, was produced in Moscow at the Ermolova Theatre in 1960. Volodin has recently been working in films.

A SMALL DOOR
TO SOVIET DRAMATURGY

BY HAROLD CLURMAN

ALEKSANDR VOLODIN'S *Five Evenings* is a simple play, so simple in fact that audiences in our great metropolitan centers might call it "corny." In doing this they would betray their own provinciality. For they would ignore the relationship of the play's material to its source, that is, to the people for whom it was first presented and whom it reflects.

Understood in this light, *Five Evenings* is wholly charming. It is "primitive," it is traditional, it is above all playable. Allow me to explain.

There is no politics in this comedy. It is a love story as guileless as those common on our American stage before 1915. In such plays some trifling impediment to the union of two good people is dramatized. All through the proceedings we feel confident that they will eventually marry and live a good life of close companionship.

One superficial difference from the conventional pattern is that the main characters in *Five Evenings* are no longer youthful. They fell in love on the eve of the war; the war separated them. After the war they lost sight of one another, though not their memories or their longing for each other. When they meet again seventeen years later they are past the age of "romance."

But what really distinguishes this play from those others once turned out among us with commercial regularity is that the Soviet play is socially purposeful. In this sense it continues an enduring tradition of Russian literature and drama. Art for art's sake has always been a rarity in Russia. In either a comic or tragic vein, Griboyedev, Ostrovsky, Gogol, Turgenev, Dostoevsky, Tolstoy are fundamentally moral artists. One might go so far as to speak of their work as "propaganda." In the greatest of these men we find an unorthodox but profoundly Christian sense of life. When unperceptive but hostile critics in Russia wanted to attack Chekhov they said his work lacked purpose, he did not declare his commitments.

The goals of Soviet dramaturgy are more readily apparent than those of the earlier men and unhappily more mandatory. The Soviet writer, unlike his forebears, must be less confused by the stress of subjective turmoil, crippling doubt, shades of destructive impulse. That is why Soviet morality, particularly as it reveals itself in Soviet drama, usually seems to us as rudimentary as a fairy tale or a poster.

The merit of *Five Evenings* is that its morality is less explicit than that of most Soviet plays. All the Soviet premises and aspirations are present but they are not sloganized or set down like so many lessons learned by rote. Volodin sheds a mellow light on Soviet society and its people.

The basic assumption is that tragedy — usually ascribed to

6

social pressures — while it cannot be totally eliminated, may be overcome, certainly transcended. All the characters in *Five Evenings* are sweet people even when they are youthfully foolish or momentarily misguided. They all wish to help one another. They are healthy, energetic and endlessly good-natured. The face of evil never appears. All are learning and teaching. Everyone is trying to be educated or educating their friends. Thus they constantly seem to express themselves in apothegms and proverbs.

The effect is, except for the cynical, bracing — and also, by the way, endemically "American"! Soviet society is a *young* society, eagerly ambitious to fulfill the tasks it has set itself. At the final curtain — when the lovers have dispelled their misunderstanding — Tamara looks forward to a good life and simply says, "Oh, if only we don't have a war!"

The Soviet dramatist is always bent on showing that life is worth living, its hardships not causes for despair but part of its wonderful challenge. No limits are set on what man can accomplish. One must study, one must work: the two are organically interrelated. Science is celebrated as an instrument to unlock the treasures of the universe for the well-being of mankind. Chemistry is described in lyrical terms.

All work, no matter how unglamorous, if engaged in with the supreme goals of life in view, is honorable. There is nothing demeaning in being a truck driver, a telephone girl, a grocery clerk — especially if one uses these jobs as a step in advancement toward more demanding tasks of broader social utility. Everyone should take pride in his contribution to society while deepening his knowledge in its performance. That is heroic which best serves the general welfare. Every man and woman thus acquires some attribute of nobility.

Not everyone is talented. But we are all capable of raising ourselves to loftier heights by respect for genius such as "Lenin, Giordano Bruno, Pushkin" as one character in the play puts it. One should read. Poets are as necessary as scientists. Great writers — among them Jack London — are mentioned with reverence. For artists teach one to think, to love life, to love one another. The consummation of these ideals is what constitutes true success.

All this is conveyed in *Five Evenings* in what seem to be monosyllables. The manner is factual, concrete, innocent, and smiling. It does not strike the audience which sees it in the Soviet Union as "kid stuff." Nor is it suspected as "propaganda." It is regarded as part of the reality the audience lives and lives by.

In this connection I feel impelled to relate a personal incident. After a performance of Arbuzov's *The Irkutsk Story*, an outstanding production at the Vachtangov Theatre which I saw in Moscow three years ago, I jokingly mentioned to my interpreter that if the boy in the play, a worker at an electric plant, had not, as he says, ever kissed a girl till he fell in love at the age of twenty-five "he is not pure, merely sick!" The interpreter laughed and said "But many of our young workers are really like that" — meaning chaste.

In *Five Evenings* references to the "twist" are made as well as to loose manners, illicit affairs, promiscuity, and the like, but they are spoken of with a candor very different from either the smirk or the venom which marks similar situations in our recent comedies. Thus one gets the impression from *Five Evenings* as from other Soviet plays not only of an all-pervading personal purity in the people but also of an unfrowning Puritanism. (This may also account for its reverse: censoriousness.) We might say that this is always characteristic of a society in the process of its early growth and pressing need for material progress. But on further consideration we recognize this delicacy of feeling and statement (in no way at variance

8

with robustness) in Chekhov, even in Gorky and certainly in the older Russian writers.

There is still another sense in which *Five Evenings*, for all its modest aim and skill, is part of a national tradition. It is eminently a play for the stage. The theatre as a total event rather than drama as literature is what most attracts the Soviet playgoer. That is why reports by foreign visitors emphasize the immense superiority of Soviet productions over the quality of the new texts on which they are based.

What matters most to the Soviet public and to its critics is that the themes or material of plays be relevant to their experience and their ideals and that a body of theatre artists and craftsmen be able to make these plays glow on the stage. So while Soviet drama is supposed to conform to the requirements of so-called Socialist Realism very few plays are mounted naturalistically. What one actually witnesses are productions enlivened by a high degree of *theatricality*.

It is evident in reading *Five Evenings* that it calls for simple but imaginative scenic treatment with acting both sturdy and sensitive, natural and nuanced, above all acting of rich human texture. Such acting, I am assured by so keen an observer of acting as Stella Adler, made a performance of *Five Evenings* that she saw in Leningrad a delightful occasion in which the audience was warmed by laughter and cleansed by tears.

A similar American production would help us appreciate the spirit of Soviet dramaturgy, and better still, understand the Soviet people. Beyond that it might provide us with an affectionate and touching evening in the theatre — *a good time*.

THE PLAY

Characters

AUTHOR	TAMARA
ZOYA	SLAVA
ILYIN	KATYA

TIMOFEYEV

Time: The present   *Place:* Leningrad

SCENE 1

═══════════════════════

(*The author walks on*)

AUTHOR

It all happened in Leningrad, in a street in Leningrad, in a
house there. It started way back, long before the five evenings.
And it will go on for quite a while. Imagine it's winter. It
snows in the evenings. And the snow brings disturbing memories — of school holidays, of meetings in the front hall, of
winters past . . .

The first evening.

(*Spot on a small divan forestage, with Zoya and Ilyin sitting
there. Between them there is a turntable playing a record.
When the tune ends Zoya lifts the needle.*)

ZOYA

Mad! I'm mad to behave like this. Please don't assume from
my behavior that I'm always so easy to get.

ILYIN

All right.

ZOYA

What's all right?

ILYIN

I don't assume.

ZOYA

Some men are no good. You're different. (*pause*) It's true, it all happened so quickly. Just a week ago we didn't even know each other. And — suddenly! I can hardly believe it. It's true, I'm quite mad. You probably despise me.

ILYIN

But why, on the contrary.

ZOYA

(*showing Ilyin a fashion magazine*) Tell me, do you like her type?

ILYIN

Not bad.

ZOYA

She's the most photographed model of the lot. Now here she's all right. But here she's awful. I haven't seen her at all in the last few numbers. I expect they've had a row. But she may have married someone well off. It's better to live on one's own as a rule. With a man, you're always buying socks or meat or vodka for him. Now do tell me, what is love?

ILYIN

Nobody knows.

ZOYA

Love — it's an electric current.

ILYIN

Quite likely

ZOYA

It's not likely — it is so. When does your leave end?

ILYIN

Quite soon. (*He makes a "tut-tut" sound, thinking*) How long
have I been away? Seventeen years? And what's interesting,
there's always some sign hanging up or a billboard or a pharmacist on the corner — all exactly the same as before. My first
love, she lived over that pharmacist there. I had a room there
before the war.

ZOYA

Really? Oh, how interesting! Do tell me about your first love.
I love it when they tell me about their first love . . .

ILYIN

She was a beauty. Girls like her don't exist now. A star. Star
was her nickname.

ZOYA

Well, I wasn't all that dim either. Actually, when I was young,
I was lovely. There was a man wanting to marry me — and
what a man! But he was middle-aged. Mother talked me out
of it. So I myself got him married to a friend of mine. I met
her the other day. All dressed up! . . . And you know it
might have been me.

ILYIN

What if I were to drop in right now.

ZOYA

Where?

ILYIN

Her flat.

ZOYA

I'll challenge her to a duel.

ILYIN

We wrote to each other all through the war. There's a whole
book.

ZOYA

If she's such a star, why did you part?

ILYIN

I didn't live up to the high ideals.

ZOYA

You mean, she sent you packing?

ILYIN

No, that's how I wanted it. Besides it was all by correspondence, in the letters we wrote.

ZOYA

You find me dull. Pity! I don't know how to talk.

ILYIN

But you do. Look what a lot you've said.

ZOYA

You're different. Now tell me the answer to this sort of problem. A girl met a man. He fell madly in love with her. She wanted to spend her whole life beside him. But suddenly he upped and left her. Then she met someone else. It wasn't quite the same, but still she got used to him. And also wanted to spend her life with him. And bonk! The same thing all over again. He left. But she'd like a family. She's a woman, you know! And her self-confidence has been shaken. "What's wrong? What is it that I haven't got?" And with the third, she's lost her pride, goes running after him almost. And people say: a loose woman . . . You haven't heard a thing I said. It's gone in through one ear and out through the other.

ILYIN

I am listening. I was just thinking about what you said.

ZOYA

What were you thinking?

ILYIN

It's what happens, my dear, just like that. A sad story.

ZOYA

Of course it's sad.

16

ILYIN

(*looking out of the window*) That was our street, right there. Our own cinema. And our private sky. What a sky, mm? A winter night, but it's blue, fit to bust! No, it's dangerous to re-visit places where you were happy at nineteen. Where I suffered, where I loved, where I buried my heart.

ZOYA

Wonder what she's like now, this Star of yours?

ILYIN

You know, it isn't late. What if I were actually to look in? She may still live here!

ZOYA

Look, Sasha, you're simply making use of me.

ILYIN

(*ruffling her hair*) Why no, my dear.
(*Ilyin sits lost in thought. Then he gets up and puts his coat on.*)

ZOYA

So that's it! All quite clear.

ILYIN

I'll be back soon. I'll just look in and come back. (*He goes*)

ZOYA

You'll come back, will you! I'll send you flying down those stairs . . . Don't you dare come back!
(*Blackout. Lights up on Tamara's rooms; one larger, one smaller. The following action takes place in either room or in both.*)

AUTHOR

Tamara is alone, sitting at her table, putting her hair in curlers. (*The doorbell rings*) Tamara ignores the doorbell, because she is not expecting anyone. (*another ring*) But the outer door is not locked. (*The outer door is heard to open.*

17

There is a knock on the door of her room.) This makes her uneasy.

TAMARA

(*going to the door*) Who's there?

ILYIN'S VOICE

Tamara Vasilyevna?

TAMARA

What's the matter?

ILYIN'S VOICE

(*clowning*) Have you got a room to let?

TAMARA

What room? It's midnight!

ILYIN'S VOICE

(*aping a time check*) At the third stroke it will be ten thirty-three. Pip! Pip! Pip!

TAMARA

Will you get out and bang that door shut as you go! (*silence*) What are you doing in there?

ILYIN'S VOICE

I'll bed down by the coat rack. But in the morning, don't throw the door wide open. Gently does it.

(*Something crashes down in the hall*)

TAMARA

What's that?

ILYIN'S VOICE

The pan.

TAMARA

Hang it up again.

ILYIN'S VOICE

I have.

TAMARA

Listen, what do you want? Who are you?

(*A passport is slipped through a crack in the door*)

18

ILYIN'S VOICE

There's my passport.

TAMARA

I don't need your passport.

AUTHOR

But she took it, opened it. And remembered. And sat down, right there by the door. Then, forgetting to remove her curlers, silent, she opened the door. There she stands looking at Ilyin, so mistrustfully, so pathetically that he laughed. Took a step towards her and in spite of some resistance planted a kiss on her cheek. After a look round as though he owned the place, he hung up his coat on a hook and walked right in.

ILYIN

Well, why are you standing there? Come in. (*She does so*) Sit down.

AUTHOR

Tamara sat down at the table and Ilyin next to her.

TAMARA

No, sit over there please.

ILYIN

(*moving to another chair*) Well?

TAMARA

What?

ILYIN

How are you? How's life? How's work?

TAMARA

(*with dignity*) As far as I'm concerned, it's all right. I'm not complaining. I'm working as a foreman at the Red Triangle. The work's interesting, responsible . . .

ILYIN

(*singing quietly, significantly*)

O my darling,
Take me with you . . .

19

TAMARA

I've even forgotten the words.

ILYIN

(*singing*)

> And far away
> You'll call me wife . . .

TAMARA

I don't remember anything at all. Who would remember? It's such a long time ago. And how are you? Have you achieved what you wanted?

ILYIN

I have and I haven't. Depends how you look at it.

TAMARA

How do you look at it?

ILYIN

Oh! . . . (*with a wave of the hand*)

> My life — the iron road,
> Forever forward!

TAMARA

It means you have achieved it. Where are you working?

ILYIN

Well, if it's as interesting as all that — I'm an engineer. If the grade interests you — chief engineer.

TAMARA

(*respectfully*) Is it a large factory?

ILYIN

The Chemical Combine at Podgorsk, that's all. If the scale interests you — quite large. One of the largest in the country.

TAMARA

(*with a polite smile*) A big ship goes far. I'm all right too. I'm working. I'm working as foreman, still at that same Triangle.

ILYIN

You're somebody, you know!

TAMARA

(*with a wave of the hand*) I have to answer for everything. The discipline and the schedule and the social work. I also take an active part in all the problems that arise. And when there are just girls working together, they get so aggressive, they even let themselves go. You get a very pretty girl sitting there with her hair in a mess. "Why don't you comb it," I tell her. "Such a pretty face but you don't look after yourself." Of course I'm a party member. You get more results from the party office if you are. In short I'm living a full life. I'm not complaining.

ILYIN

Do you live alone?

TAMARA

Why alone? I live with my nephew. Lucy died during the blockade. There's no Lucy. But Slavick remained. A very gifted boy — they all say that. He's studying at the Technical School, following in your footsteps. An active boy, does other things as well. There's a social side to him too. So he's also living a full life . . . And have you come on business?

ILYIN

Not for long, three days or so.

TAMARA

Three days?

ILYIN

Or four.

TAMARA

Or four. Well, then do stay with us, if you like. Slava will sleep on the camp bed. He won't bother you much. There is just one condition — you're not to bring anyone in. The boy is studying. I'm tired when I get home. What we value most is

21

peace and quiet. (*Ilyin brings out his cigarettes and lights one*) Do you smoke?

ILYIN

(*with a laugh*) I still smoke.

TAMARA

I forgot. Do smoke, but open the top window. (*She goes out into the hall to fetch the camp bed*)

AUTHOR

Ilyin pocketed his cigarettes and got up. He looked into the room where he lived once upon a time. He stood there. He went back to the coat rack, took down his coat. And in the hall met Tamara.

ILYIN

All right, sleep well.

TAMARA

Where are you going?

ILYIN

I shan't trouble you. Go to bed, it's late . . . We've had our meeting.

TAMARA

(*hurriedly, but still retaining her official tone*) You won't be any trouble. No trouble at all. You'll be comfortable here. Do have a look. (*She opens the door of the other room and turns on the light*) The bed's clean. I only changed it today. I don't know, you must decide what's best for you. I'm not going to persuade you to stay . . .

ILYIN

(*wavers, then returns*) Thank you. (*He goes to her*)

TAMARA

(*just as hurriedly, but with returning dignity*) You can go to bed now, it's late, so I'll say good-night.

ILYIN

Good-night. (*He goes into the small room*)

22

AUTHOR

Tamara closed the door after him, made sure that the door was closed. Sat down on the bed, threw both hands up to her hair — a habit of hers — felt the curlers sticking out, glanced into the mirror and gasped with shame. She removed the curlers one by one and flung them at the wall. (*Disturbed, Ilyin opens the door*)

TAMARA

(*turning round, shouting*) If you're going to open the door at night will you please knock! Is that understood?

ILYIN

Broadly speaking — yes. (*He closes the door again*)

AUTHOR

Tamara grandly stalked to the switch, turned off the light, went back to bed, flung herself down flat, and burying her face in the pillow quieted down. It's dark in the room except for the faint glow of the street lamps reflected in the windows. (*There is a not very loud bang of the outer door, a click of the key in the inner door. The light is switched on.*) That's Slava and Katya. They come in their coats with their collars up. They listen. It's quiet where Tamara is lying behind the screen.

KATYA

It isn't convenient. I'd better go home.

SLAVA

(*feeling embarrassed*) Not convenient? What do you know? (*He looks into the sideboard*) There! Food. (*He places a stick of bread and round of sausage on the table. He helps Katya out of her coat. He removes the newspapers from the drawing board.*) Take a look at this. Quite a job! (*Katya bends over it*) Careful. (*He covers it up again. They sit down at the table, break off some bread, and take turns biting the sausage.*) There's primitive communism for you!

23

KATYA

Interesting, but has there been a primitive Young Communist? (*taking a look at Tamara's bookshelf*) What a lot of books you have! Have you read *The Scorpion?* There's a woman drawn on the cover, with a wineglass and, you know . . . half naked.

SLAVA

No, I haven't.

KATYA

God, what murk! . . . A footballer lent it to me. I have contacts in the world of sport, you know. I can get passes for all the matches.

SLAVA

I can see you get around.

KATYA

So what! I know lots of people. I'm used to boy friends. I was friends with a boy for two years after I left school. I even met the son of a general once. Word of honor! He said so himself, first thing: "I'm the son of a general."

SLAVA

What a liar you are!

KATYA

(*not offended*) It's true! Even foreigners like me. The Swedes. Remember when the Swedes came? I met a seaman.

SLAVA

He had a couple of hours on shore, so he threw himself at the first girl who came along.

KATYA

Well, yes. He kissed my hand. Asked for my permission and kissed it.

SLAVA

What are you so pleased about? (*After looking at the screen,*

24

he moves his chair up to Katya and embraces her rather awk-
wardly but with great determination)

KATYA

(*for a moment at a loss, then talking quickly*) Auntie made
herself an orange frock. People used to turn and stare in the
street at her. She's old. So she's given it to me.

SLAVA

Do you want people to turn and stare at you too?

KATYA

If they do, they'll only say okay. (*She gives Slava a tight little
smile, removes his hand from her shoulder, and gently but
stubbornly puts it on his knee)*

SLAVA

I don't get it.

KATYA

In the garden yesterday I saw a she-sparrow drag a he-
sparrow by the wing. He must have been unfaithful to her
. . . (*Slava gets up, finds Tamara's cigarettes, lights one.
Returning to Katya, he stands behind her. She tidies her hair.*)
I'm going to have my hair dyed, because I've never been a
brunette, not once. (*She gets up, faces him, and laughs anxiously*)

SLAVA

When I look at you, I wonder if you're a fool or if you're
wise.

KATYA

Neither fool, nor wise. I'm fun. I'm asked out specially because I am such fun.

SLAVA

(*embracing her from behind*) And have you had lots of fun?

KATYA

(*smiling at first, then angry — unclasping his hands with diffi-
culty*) Can't you keep your hands to yourself?

SLAVA

(*bristling*) What have I done?

KATYA

Nothing. But if everyone were to let their hands do what they like . . .

SLAVA

What am I? Everyone?

KATYA

Did you think you had special privileges? Try the dances at the Marble Hall. The little scarecrows there will suit you down to the ground.

SLAVA

Why come to the cinema with me? You meet a man for the first time . . .

KATYA

I know my way around. What's wrong with going to the cinema?

SLAVA

(*painfully casual*) What's wrong with this? (*He embraces her*)

KATYA

(*breaks away*) How much was the ticket?

SLAVA

(*goodnatured*) Four fifty.

KATYA

(*putting the money on the table*) There you are, and another fifty, the tip. (*She makes for the door*)

TAMARA

(*moving the screen and sitting up in bed*) It's midnight. You have to be up at eight tomorrow.

KATYA

(*to Tamara*) I am very sorry. (*to Slava*) And another thing,

I have met you before. I share a flat with your Lidochka. That's how observant you are.

TAMARA

Look here, young woman! You've come to see a young man at his home in the middle of the night. You're too young to behave like that. And trying to distract Slava from his studies.

KATYA

I'm not distracting him. It's not because of me that he gets two out of ten.

TAMARA

What two out of ten?

KATYA

Why don't you ask his Lidochka?

TAMARA

What Lidochka? (*to Slava*) What's all this about?

SLAVA

How should I know?

KATYA

No one likes her in the flat. That copy cat of yours.

TAMARA

What copy cat?

KATYA

Very quick at taking down lecture notes, word for word, like a parrot. But it's just too bad, Slava's quarreled with her. She's stopped giving them to him. But when she needs anything, he does all he can even if it lands him in trouble. No one likes her in the flat. She won't answer the door. Lean on the doorbell, if you like. All she ever does is leaf through her notebooks. So I call her copy cat or the everlasting pen.

TAMARA

Well, really, she's obviously a painstaking, serious young woman. And it wouldn't do you any harm to follow her example.

KATYA

Why should I? I'm doing very well as I am.

TAMARA

What an answer! You're a young woman. Your honor should come first. I was bringing him up, when I was your age.

SLAVA

It's started.

TAMARA

What?

SLAVA

I say it's time to go to bed.

TAMARA

As for you! How could you! Coming home together. At midnight!

KATYA

We got frozen in the front hall. We came up to get warm.

TAMARA

(*not listening*) You should be ashamed of yourself! Bringing her here, to my flat.

KATYA

But where should he take me to, a friend?

TAMARA

Do go away. I want to go to sleep.

KATYA

Good-night.

TAMARA

Rattle the bolt, the porter will let you out.

SLAVA

(*grimly*) I'll see you home.

KATYA

I can find my way. (*She goes*)

TAMARA

Slava, what's happened?

28

SLAVA

Such a lark, you know. Lida and I decided we'd go to the exam together and I had the cribs to the questions.

TAMARA

What cribs?

SLAVA

What does it matter! Numbered cribs, thirty in each pocket. She took a question, thirty-one. (*getting excited*) So I started going through the right pocket, got to thirty, realized that thirty-one was in the left pocket. Well, I found her the crib eventually and started looking for my own. I brought it out and instead of number nine, it was eleven . . .

TAMARA

But what were you doing with the cribs?

SLAVA

Didn't you ever study anything?

TAMARA

I studied without cribs.

SLAVA

Ostrich-idealist.

TAMARA

Perhaps. Now will you tell me what this girl is?

SLAVA

Well, from trunks exchange, a telephonist.

TAMARA

And she agreed to come home with you after your first meeting? At night?

SLAVA

She may have relied on my being a decent type.

TAMARA

That's the last thing she worries about. You know what women there are! Be honest with me, doesn't it fill you with disgust?

SLAVA

No.

TAMARA

My God, that's what you're like! No principles!

SLAVA

You have too many principles! That's why you aren't married.

TAMARA

(*getting out of bed, very upset*) Yes, it is because of principles . . . all because of principles. As for you, you're insolent. There's nothing sacred for you. And you consider that an achievement. "Look at me, I'm not afraid of anything!" you say. (*She takes down a book from the shelf and opens it*) Here, I want you to read this.

SLAVA

All right, put it down.

TAMARA

No, now, in my presence.

SLAVA

I'm saturated with reading to the marrow of my bones. I'm full up with theory.

TAMARA

(*looks at him in silence, then smacks him hard on the cheek*) These are the letters of Karl Marx! (*She again lies down on the bed, her face in the pillow*)

(*Ilyin enters*)

SLAVA

Who's that?

ILYIN

Ilyin, Aleksandr Petrovich.

SLAVA

What Ilyin?

30

ILYIN

I'm staying with you for a while.

SLAVA

A pleasure.

TAMARA

Why hide it from me that you got two out of ten? You told a girl whom you don't know but you hid it from me!

SLAVA

I haven't told anything to anyone. And I don't like discussing my affairs before strangers.

TAMARA

He's not a stranger. He knew you when you were two years old. Let him listen.

(*Ilyin props himself up against the doorway and listens*)

SLAVA

The tragedy of the life of a Soviet student — "The Start of the Road." Attention! Curtain up!

TAMARA

I gave up my whole youth to him! There's nothing left!

ILYIN

All right, old man, it's time you went to bed.

(*Slava takes the camp bed and goes into his room*)

TAMARA

(*to Ilyin*) You too! Go away! I'm fed up with both of you. (*Ilyin turns to go*) But first lock the door. (*Ilyin locks the outer door*) And put the light out. (*He puts the light out*) At least let me have some sleep tonight!

(*Ilyin goes into the other room, sits on the divan. Slava clatters around with the camp bed, getting in the way of the guest as much as possible.*)

ILYIN

Well, how's that Technical School of ours? Is Fomichev alive?

SLAVA

Fulminating. Why, are you a victim of science too?

ILYIN

A victim, in actual fact. I was chucked out in my third year.

SLAVA

What for?

ILYIN

My frankness. There was an occasion when I took my time and explained to Fomichev exactly what I thought of him. So he waged a cold war against me which he concluded with a brilliant victory at the end of the year.

SLAVA

It's what happens.

ILYIN

I see you don't get on with your aunt.

SLAVA

According to Newton's third law to every action there is an equal and contrary reaction. So she educates me and I resist.

ILYIN

Tell me, has she always lived alone? Didn't she marry?

SLAVA

The unfortunate man hasn't been born yet . . . Actually, there was someone in the hazy dawn of her youth. According to unofficial data.

ILYIN

Quiet! (*with a nod toward the door*) You know, it was probably me. We met before the war. I used to rent this room here. Your father was in the navy. Your mother and Toma had just started working at the Triangle. She was a beauty, your aunt. Girls like that don't exist now. A star! That's what they called her at the workshop: Star. She'd come running from the factory, tap-tap on the stairs . . .

SLAVA

But you're a romantic.

ILYIN

We corresponded right through the war. Then, owing to certain circumstances, I stopped writing, but I carted her letters around with me. Then even her letters got lost somewhere.

SLAVA

You know, in your place, I'd write a poem about it. Something like that:

> The dear glance of your eyes divine,
> Aroused my heart's ardor.
> Of all the girls you alone are mine,
> Enshrined in my heart's arbor.

ILYIN

(*laughs*) Not bad, except for that last rhyme.

SLAVA

Rhymes are not important. As long as you feel it here. (*He thumps his chest*) Well, I'm glad we've met. (*He holds out his hand to Ilyin, who slowly squeezes it until Slava gasps*)

ILYIN

Ssh . . . ssh . . . (*He squeezes it some more and Slava half rises*) Ssh . . . ssh . . . (*with deadly calm*) So there. If you offend that woman in my presence, I'll flay the seven skins off your back, and naked into Africa off you pack. How's that for a rhyme?

SLAVA

(*with a groan*) It will do.

ILYIN

Ssh . . . ssh . . . (*He lets Slava go*) What's the date today?

SLAVA

The fifteenth.

ILYIN

Well then, during the days I'm spending here in your house, I intend to see that that woman is happy. Got that?

SLAVA

Got that. (*He takes a towel and goes into the kitchen*)

(*Ilyin puts out the light. In the semi-darkness we can see Tamara and Ilyin. They are lying in their rooms with their eyes wide open.*)

ILYIN

Toma . . . (*Tamara does not answer*) Toma . . . (*Tamara is silent*) Toma! (*pause*)

TAMARA

What?

ILYIN

You awake? (*pause*) I used to think about you. And you?

TAMARA

I used to at first.

ILYIN

You haven't changed much.

TAMARA

Stop chattering. (*Ilyin starts whistling the tune*) That's enough, I've got to go to work early.

ILYIN

Good-night.

TAMARA

Good-night.

(*They are lying there with their eyes wide open. Slow blackout.*)

SCENE 2

AUTHOR

So ended the first evening.

The second evening. We'll go on with the second evening immediately because nothing important happened during the day.

(*Ilyin and Slava are in Tamara's room. Ilyin is sitting astride a chair, watching Slava. During the following conversation Slava lays a white tablecloth on the table, places three little bunches of mimosa in glass jars around the room, and wipes the dust off the chest of drawers.*)

ILYIN

You see how nice it is. With a white tablecloth and flowers on the table you feel embarrassed if you're petty, rude, bad tempered. The tablecloth should have folds ironed in. The folds bring back childhood memories.

SLAVA

How grand.

ILYIN

You must live wisely, without any fuss. Know that in the book of life there are many superfluous details. But the secret is that you can skip those pages.

SLAVA

Well, there you are, I have no wish to read this particular page. After all, Aunt Toma can do the clearing up when she comes. There's division of labor, isn't there?

ILYIN

(*politely*) Don't make me angry, go on working. (*Without replying Slava sits down on another chair in the same way as Ilyin*) And you're going to perform this operation every Saturday.

SLAVA

Ha-ha.

ILYIN

Now get up. (*Slava does not move*) It's uncomfortable hitting someone who's sitting down. (*Slava gets up. So does Ilyin.*) Drop your chin right down, on your chest, stand sideways to the enemy, with your left arm well forward, your right defending your chin. You can't be hit in this fighter position. (*Slava takes up the position*) The most effective blows are those inflicted on the end of the chin. You don't swing your arm in boxing. The trajectory of the fist is along a straight line, since the straight line is the shortest distance between two points. Got that?

SLAVA

Got that.

ILYIN

Jab! (*Slava hits out. Ilyin puts out the palm of his hand, taking a step back.*) Left forward, bring up the right. Punch!

36

(*the same*) Fingers down, short, sudden, jab! (*moving toward the door*) Jab!

(*The door opens behind him. It's Katya in an orange frock. For a moment she looks on in silence, then suddenly with a penetrating shriek she hurls herself on Ilyin, hanging onto his arm.*)

KATYA

What are you doing, you crawling viper! What are you doing!

SLAVA

You balmy? Let him go. That hold is not allowed. (*Katya lets Ilyin go*) We're training, understand? Boxing technique.

KATYA

(*to Ilyin*) You know what you get with this training? Fifteen days.

ILYIN

You fiendish woman. Have you had a manicure, or what?

KATYA

(*to Slava*) Why did you come to the exchange?

SLAVA

I was just passing — I looked in.

KATYA

And I thought — on business. Don't come otherwise. (*She turns toward the door*)

SLAVA

Why don't you sit down for a bit?

KATYA

What next!

SLAVA

What's the hurry . . .

KATYA

My little ones are crying for their mother.

SLAVA

Aleksandr Petrovich, don't you think she looks like Carmen?

KATYA

(*flattered, though it is not at all true*) It's not true. But they do say I look like actress Larionova – it's possible.

SLAVA

(*to Ilyin*) Well, yes, there is a likeness.

KATYA

I don't know. Others say I look like the Fyodorov sisters. But somehow I'm losing weight. Last year my waist was twenty-eight, now it's twenty-six and a half. I'm quite emaciated.

SLAVA

Why's that?

KATYA

I've fallen deeply in love.

SLAVA

Who with? Not a secret, is it?

KATYA

With our fitter, Vanya.

SLAVA

I see you're all dressed up. (*to Ilyin*) No, young girls shouldn't wear bright colors. They should at least pretend they're out of this world. All right, since you've come, get with it. We need distracting.

KATYA

What are all these preparations?

ILYIN

It's a celebration. A birthday.

KATYA

(*with a nod at Slava*) Not his, is it?

ILYIN

No, not his . . . his aunt's.

KATYA

How old does that make her?

38

SLAVA

A birthday is abstract as a rule.

KATYA

I get it. Incidentally, there's a woman on our floor who's thirty-eight. She got married.

SLAVA

To a man of seventy.

KATYA

At thirty-eight you'd marry anything.

ILYIN

Now, down to business. Dust the window, the little shelf. There's two of you now. Get on with it. I'll be back soon. (*He goes*)

KATYA

(*takes off her coat and puts on an apron*) First they set the table, then they start dusting. Domestic helps all over!

SLAVA

All right, more work and less talk. (*He sits on Ilyin's chair and watches her work*)

KATYA

(*after a pause*) I was walking down the street just now and saw two birds sitting under a ledge. He was asleep and she was pecking him — she was bored. (*Slava is silent. Katya looks out of the window.*) Look, there's a girl wearing bootees. They cost three hundred roubles. It would be all right if they cost a hundred and fifty. I'd certainly buy a pair.

SLAVA

Aunt Toma has a women's calendar. It calculates that in an average life of seventy years, sleep takes up twenty-five years, eating six, washing oneself one and a half years. But if you were to calculate how much time is spent in nonsensical talk . . .

KATYA

You don't have to talk. (*She tidies up in silence. Dusting the bookshelf, she picks up a book and opens it.*) Jules Renard.

SLAVA

It won't interest you.

KATYA

Why not! (*She puts the book aside on a small table and continues working in silence*) I may be a student too. I have contacts at the Technical School. I may go there, it's almost like the institute, four years of study.

SLAVA

Come on, concentrate.

KATYA

And why not, when our fitter says I have technical ability. It's rare in women. I had very good reports in school — that I was an angel. Only I'd rather not leave the exchange. I haven't been ticked off once all this time, only thanked. Because they all know me, that I work well. When I'm on duty, even my voice is different, isn't it? (*pause*) Slava, do you want to go and see "The Dawn" at eight-thirty? I know the girl at the box office. Once I brought two boys with me. I sat between them and one said: "You came with me, turn towards me." I turned towards him and the other one started having pretensions.

SLAVA

And shall I be the third one sitting there? You'll be doing the twist. (*pointing*) Now, go and tidy the other room.

(*Katya goes into Slava's room. Tamara enters. She looks at the preparations in silence.*)

TAMARA

What's going on here? Who allowed you to use that tablecloth? Why have you put the jars out? They have to go back to the shop. I put them aside specially. Will you get off that chair and explain to me what it's all about . . .

40

SLAVA

How should I know . . . It was your lodger who gave the orders.

TAMARA

(*after a pause*) What has my lodger got to do with it! He should thank me for letting him spend the night here. What next? Imposing his rule on an alien monastery. Empty those jars. (*Slava piles the mimosa on the windowsill. Tamara removes the tablecloth. The room gradually acquires its old look. Katya appears in the door. Tamara starts with fright.*) Who's that?

KATYA

It's me, Katya.

TAMARA

And what good fortune brings you here?

KATYA

I . . . I just came.

TAMARA

On your own? (*Katya looks down, vaguely shrugging her shoulders*) And what were you doing in there?

KATYA

Dusting the trunk.

TAMARA

(*to Slava*) Push it back in its place.

SLAVA

Shall I put the rubbish back too?
(*Ilyin enters and stops by the door. He is carrying various parcels and a bottle of wine.*)

ILYIN

(*to Slava*) What's the matter? Will you put the flowers back. (*Slava is enjoying these contradictory orders. He swaggers off towards the flowers and replaces them in the jars.*)

41

TAMARA

(*watches him in silence*) Will you empty those jars. I have to
return them to the shop.

(*Slava chuckles and waits for further orders*)

ILYIN

(*to Tamara*) We decided to wash it down.

TAMARA

Wash what down?

ILYIN

Our meeting.

TAMARA

First, I don't see any need for a fireworks display to our meeting. Secondly, I have to change.

ILYIN

In that case I apologize. (*to Slava*) Empty the jars. Put the
food in the larder, the flowers in the dustbin. (*He goes into
the next room*)

(*Tamara stands thinking*)

SLAVA

Aunt Toma, you've really gone too far.

TAMARA

Do you think I've offended him?

SLAVA

And how! A man goes to a lot of trouble, and then you . . .

TAMARA

I don't know. All right, call him if you like.

SLAVA

You threw him out, call him yourself.

TAMARA

(*after a pause*) Maybe he really was offended. (*quietly to
Slava*) What's her name?

SLAVA

Yekaterina.

42

TAMARA

Katya, call him, if you'd like to . . .

KATYA

It would be rather tactless for me to call him. I'm a guest myself.

(*Tamara stands for a while undecided, then opens the door
of the other room*)

TAMARA

Aleksandr Petrovich! You aren't offended, are you? Well, if
you like, do let's have a drink. Why all the fuss! . . . (*She
goes out into the kitchen*)

KATYA

Isn't she peculiar!

SLAVA

In the world, my friend, there's a lot that's incomprehensible.
(*He puts glasses on the table and sits down*) Gong for grub!
(*Katya — cool and impenetrable — also sits down, with the
book by Renard she had been leafing through during the pre-
ceding dialogue. Slava opens the bottle and pours himself out
a glass.*) Later on they won't give us any.

KATYA

(*putting her hand over her glass*) I mustn't. It upsets me.

SLAVA

We don't hold with teetotalers. Here goes! (*He swallows,
chokes, but is not put out*) Cheers!

KATYA

(*indifferently*) Have some bread and butter with it.

(*Tamara returns and sees the opened bottle*)

TAMARA

You couldn't wait, could you?

SLAVA

Katya and I are epicureans. Do you know what was written
over their doors? "Enter, passer-by, delights await you here."

KATYA

What a disgusting thing to say.

TAMARA

They meant spiritual, not carnal delights.

SLAVA

Then I recant. I'd rather be a stoic.

TAMARA

Isn't it time you were a Marxist?

SLAVA

Even Marx wasn't born a Marxist. He became a Marxist later.

TAMARA

Then go into the kitchen and make some salad.

SLAVA

What salad? What's salad got to do with it?

TAMARA

(*loudly*) Aleksandr Petrovich, will you tell him!

SLAVA

Well, you know . . . (*But he goes*)

TAMARA

Let's move the table toward the divan, shall we, and dance? I haven't danced in a hundred years, I've forgotten how. Nowadays it's done in style, isn't it?

KATYA

Not necessarily. It depends.

(*They talk as they set the table*)

TAMARA

Will there be room enough for you and Slava?

KATYA

Yes, only I'm not sitting next to him!

TAMARA

Why not?

KATYA

Because . . . It's true what they say — that the overeducated

44

are worse than the undereducated. We spent the whole evening together and didn't talk about anything very much.

TAMARA

Perhaps he's bored with you.

KATYA

He'd cheer up immediately, if I wanted it. He's already had one or two goes but without success.

TAMARA

It's your own fault. It means he doesn't have much respect for you.

KATYA

Fancy! What a superman! I read more than he does. If you don't believe me, I'll bring my notebook and show it to you. It's where I write down various ideas.

TAMARA

My dear, you'll never catch up with him. He's a student.

KATYA

So what? Have you read *Martin Eden*? He learned it all in a few months, even the political books. Do you know how I read? I can read sixty pages in an hour. Seventy, if it's verse.

TAMARA

What's the good of that? Better read a page and think about it. Otherwise what you read today you forget tomorrow.

KATYA

Yes, but you don't know what a memory I've got! I only have to read something twice and I know it by heart. I already know Aleksandr Tvardovsky by heart, Aleksandr Blok, Aleksei Surkov . . .

SLAVA

(*entering with a bowl of salad*) Vera Panova, Vera Ketlinskaya, Vera Inber . . .

KATYA

(*loudly*) Aleksandr Petrovich, will you tell him!

45

TAMARA

Slava, you really are so bad-tempered.

KATYA

If people were not so bad-tempered, they'd see the loveliness that surrounds them.

SLAVA

I've read that somewhere.

KATYA

Jules Renard.

TAMARA

You're always reading what you're not supposed to, but you never have time to study. Do you want to get another two out of ten?

SLAVA

I don't have the lecture notes on thermodynamics. I'll borrow some tomorrow and then I'll get down to it.

KATYA

(*to Tamara*) How can one use other people's notes!

(*Ilyin enters*)

TAMARA

Aleksandr Petrovich, will you tell him! . . .

ILYIN

Why, yes, stands to reason. Taking down lecture notes, brother, is not a mechanical process. You're learning at the same time.

SLAVA

There goes the second front.

ILYIN

The celebrations are dragging a bit, let's have a drink, shall we?

SLAVA

(*drinking*) Here's how!

46

KATYA

Oh, do let's have something to eat!

SLAVA

Feed her.

KATYA

It's not me that I'm worried about. If you must know, I've already been to a party today.

SLAVA

(*taking her plate away*) Oh, she's already been to a party today.

TAMARA

Slava!

KATYA

I don't mind. On the whole I don't believe in boys anymore. I had a boy friend for two years. Then he beat me up and left me. In past centuries you laid down your life for a girl. No, that's not possible now. Nowadays there's a swing in the opposite direction. They aren't interested in a girl who's going to discuss ideas with them. They have one aim — they've simply got to reach a certain objective. If he goes home without a kiss, it means the evening's been wasted.

TAMARA

It also depends on the girl. You must be proud.

(*Slava puts a record on. He invites Katya to dance. Tamara glances at Ilyin, raises her glass to him, and they drink.*)

SLAVA

What utter rubbish! I blame you, and everyone will blame you because you've been drinking on your own without a toast. Katya, let's drink to our fraternal friendship!

TAMARA

Pipe down, you're beside yourself.

SLAVA

Why should I, I'm enjoying myself, I'm not ashamed of it. Incidentally I'm not enjoying myself as much as you think. Aunt Toma! (*He kisses her cheek*) I'm the only one who understands you. You can rely on me!

ILYIN

(*putting Slava's glass aside*) You've had more than enough. Go and have a rest.

SLAVA

I don't know what to do. To withdraw significantly or to remain significantly.

KATYA

(*politely to Ilyin*) And why are you ordering him about? Who are you but a lodger. A lodger. It means you must behave tactfully. You have a bad influence on Slava too. He's had three glasses. What's it for?

(*pause*)

AUTHOR

He doesn't answer her, nor does Tamara. They aren't listening to her. They're sitting there, on this second evening, lost in memories, his hand on hers.

(*Slava attracts Katya's attention to this answer to her question. He nods in the direction of the door, conveys to her to go, that he will join her. Katya moves away quietly, puts her coat on and goes. Then Slava also gets up and quietly makes for the door.*)

TAMARA

(*glancing toward Slava*) And where's Katya?

SLAVA

She's gone home.

TAMARA

Where are you off to?

SLAVA

I'm going for a walk.

TAMARA

Can't you see it's night outside? Sit down.

(*Slava sits down on a chair near the door. Tamara takes a guitar and strums. Slava gets up and takes his coat.*)

ILYIN

You were told to sit down.

SLAVA

(*sitting down with a sigh*) There they go again.

TAMARA

(*Slava slips out as she sings.*)

> O my darling, take me with you,
> and far away you'll call me wife.
> O my love, I'd take you with me,
> but far away I have a wife.
> O my darling, take me with you,
> and far away you'll call me sister.
> O my love, I'd take you with me,
> but far away I have a sister.
> O my darling, take me with you,
> and far away you'll call me stranger.
> O my love, I'd take you with me,
> but far away I need no stranger.

(*suddenly speaking very simply*) How awful it would be, if I'd married someone else.

ILYIN

What? (*Tamara plays louder and louder and faster and faster*) What did you say?

(*Slow blackout. Now the orchestra takes up the music, which sounds purposeful, passionate, and almost exotic.*)

SCENE 3

AUTHOR

The third evening.

It's growing dark. The evening shift has taken over. It is still snowing. Porters are putting down sand on the icy paths between the piles of snow but women and children turn them slippery again. The parks and gardens are as quiet as a forest. And the fortress of St. Peter and St. Paul appears to stand, not on the bank of the river, but on the very edge of a snow-field.

(*Trunks exchange. Forestage. A small barrier with Katya at the switchboard beyond it. Slava is sitting on a bench. Two telephone kiosks, numbers 5 and 4, are painted on the back-drop. The other kiosks are in the wings. We don't see the subscribers but hear their conversations from the wings.*)

KATYA

(*speaking with the intonations of telephonists*) Hullo! Exchange? Three seven, Seryozha, fifteen minutes . . . Minsk! Minsk, in number three! (*During the pauses in the following scene, Katya can carry on with her work and talk into the microphone*) Time's up. Have you finished? . . . Zvenigorod? I want Kubinka, it's a village . . . Fifty-three, who's taking it? . . . Murom in number four, Murom in number four . . . Have you finished? I'm disconnecting you, that's the lot, that's all . . .

VOICE FROM A KIOSK IN THE WINGS

Daddy, I want to talk with Mummy. Is that you, Mummy? It's all right, five teeth. Two upper and three lower.

SLAVA

And one in the middle.

KATYA

If you're going to laugh, go and laugh in the street. Vyborg, in number three, go and take your call please.

GIRL'S VOICE

Seryozha? Did you receive my letter? No, you tell me, did you receive my letter?

SLAVA

He's lying, of course he received her letter.

GIRL'S VOICE

Then why didn't you answer? No, you go on. Go on and talk, I've booked fifteen minutes. I got my grant.

KATYA

I thought you said you wouldn't come here again.

SLAVA

I came to phone.

KATYA

Go ahead.

51

SLAVA

I need some change.

KATYA

What do you take me for — the cashier? (*She flings down a coin*)

SLAVA

Shall I pull myself together and give Lidochka a ring? (*He gets his number*) Lidochka? It's Slava. Hullo to you! What are your plans for this evening? . . . How about "The Dawn" at eight-thirty? Don't be such a hypocrite. You've just handed it in today. You can do some more work tomorrow . . .

KATYA

I told you, you need a student who knows the answer to A plus B. (*Slava puts down the receiver*) But the student doesn't need you. (*on her phone*) Hullo? Vanya? I'm glad you phoned, I was getting bored. Today? I don't know, I haven't really thought . . . Me? When? Well, remind me where, what, and when? But I have no intention of proving it. Oh, all right, I'll come. But aren't you the pessimist? All right, so I met a man here. I nearly died of boredom. He showed me his working drawings, to show off . . .

SLAVA

> The fitter was called Ivan,
> At heart quite a Parisian,
> He called himself Don Juan,
> Don Juan, the electrician.

KATYA

What's it got to do with you? Petrozavodsk, in number three.

OFFICIAL

(*offstage, speaking very fast*) Pestrikov? I've dispatched the duraluminium, invoice seven-four-four-o. Now listen, I've collected two lots of apparatus, they've promised to deliver the third lot. Is that clear? Good. Then that's all. Till tomorrow.

KATYA

You see, people get on with their business, while you just sit here. Go and study.

(*A woman's laugh is heard, coming from the street. Ilyin and Tamara enter. She is laughing, shaking the snow off.*)

TAMARA

(*to Ilyin*) There, you see, what did I tell you. He's again hanging around here. (*to Slava*) She's working! And it wouldn't hurt you to go and do some work yourself.

KATYA

Don't worry, he won't come again. But if he's a fly-by-night, then I'm going to have fun.

TAMARA

(*to Slava*) Apologize to her.

SLAVA

Why should I?

ILYIN

There's nothing humiliating about apologizing to a girl. It's always worse for them than it is for us.

TAMARA

I'm glad you think so, though it isn't true. At the moment you're all worse off than I am. I've seen summer lightning in the sky. That's lucky.

SLAVA

Summer lightning doesn't occur in winter.

TAMARA

But if I saw it! If I saw it with my own eyes, what then?

ILYIN

Then it does occur.

TAMARA

Do you understand?

53

SLAVA

What is there to understand?

TAMARA

You'll learn! Let's go, I'm awfully hungry.

ILYIN

I'll join you. But I must make a phone call. (*Tamara and Slava go. Ilyin sits down and dials.*) Inquiries? The number of the Gastronome, corner of Liteyny and Pestel. Yes, thank you. (*getting through*) May I speak to Zoya in the grocery department? . . . Zoya? Hullo, it's Sasha. I promised to come round. I'm sorry, I can't. No, I can't tomorrow. I can't later on, either.

(*Blackout. Lights up on Tamara's room. This time it's ready for a celebration. A light tablecloth, flowers. Slava is sitting gloomily at the writing table, drowning in textbooks and lecture notes. Tamara, wearing a dressy frock, is sitting sideways on the windowsill, excitedly watching Ilyin, who stands in the middle of the room.*)

ILYIN

(*with appropriate gestures*) Oklahoma, cinerama, pneumothorax, guadarama! (*He removes from under Slava's collar an orange and presents it to Tamara. Delighted, she eats it.*) Allez-oop! . . . (*From Slava's ear he pulls out a transparent scarf and throws it over Tamara*)

SLAVA

To Allah with you both, the further the better! I have to work. (*He takes out of his pocket a bottle of perfume and a bar of chocolate*)

ILYIN

(*rolling up his sleeves*) Stool pigeon!

TAMARA

Aleksandr Petrovich is leaving. We must celebrate.

54

SLAVA

Without me. (*He picks up his books and goes into the other room*)

(*Immediately the room feels quiet and empty. A long pause. Thrusting his hands in his pockets, Ilyin spins round the room and goes up to Tamara.*)

ILYIN

You have beautiful hands.

TAMARA

All women have beautiful hands.

ILYIN

Do you remember the front hall?

TAMARA

Don't I just!

ILYIN

We spent a lot of time there.

TAMARA

We were mad. Do you remember kissing me the first time? Right on the stairs. Oh! I was so frightened, I dropped my bag. (*Ilyin takes a step toward her. She rises, leans against the wall, looking down. They kiss. The book in her hand falls on the floor.*) Why does everyone kiss in the front hall? As though we've all been sentenced to do just that. Tell me, why?

ILYIN

I don't know.

TAMARA

Because it's warm there. (*They kiss. There is a knock on the door from the other room.*) Why are you knocking?

(*Slava enters, takes something from the writing table, and goes without raising his eyes*)

ILYIN

You have beautiful eyes.

TAMARA

Just large eyes, a large size.

ILYIN

And you have a good complexion.

TAMARA

Now, really! It's true that I used to have a good complexion. I got on the tram today and heard: "There's a seat here, mum." I looked round. It was addressed to me.

ILYIN

Yes, time flies. The older we get, the faster it goes. (*taking her head in his hands*) Are you my life or have I dreamed it! Still, youth is a damnable thing. Full of broken promises, nothing but broken promises. And we go on believing those promises.

TAMARA

There were no broken promises in my case. I always knew I'd be happy. And now I am happy!

ILYIN

That's all right. It's a large world, I shan't fall off.

TAMARA

I knew, I always knew that you'd go far. Chief engineer. That means production manager. I have a section with eighty girls under me. But you have a combine, a whole town! Do the workmen like you?

ILYIN

I don't know, I haven't asked.

TAMARA

They can't all like you – it never happens. But most of them like you, of course. I'm sure of that.

ILYIN

(*coming to a decision*) Toma, there's something I must tell you. But it's between ourselves.

TAMARA

Between ourselves . . . Only between ourselves. Between you and me.

ILYIN

Toma, I want to leave my job.

TAMARA

How do you mean, leave? Why?

ILYIN

I'm fed up with it.

TAMARA

I don't understand. Do you mean that?

ILYIN

Absolutely.

TAMARA

Why do you have such strange thoughts? Are you tired, perhaps? Doing the work you do, you live in a muddle. And when a man's on his own, generally speaking, everything seems so depressing. It will be different from now on. Do believe me. It's only five hours away, no distance at all.

ILYIN

You don't understand. I'm fed up with it! . . . One must gamble against fate with large stakes. Either you win or fate wins.

TAMARA

(*anxious*) Has something gone wrong? Are you in trouble?

ILYIN

Really, how odd people are! Does something have to go wrong?

TAMARA

I simply thought that you liked your work so much, you've talked so much about it . . .

ILYIN

Oh! . . . (*with a wave of the hand*) Listen, Toma! Let's

57

uproot ourselves, let's wander off somewhere north. I'm a first-class driver, here's my license! (*He takes the license out of his pocket and waves it*) I'm a driver and a mechanic. Well? Would you think less of me, or not? (*Tamara is silent, gathering her thoughts*) Answer my question. I'm interested.

TAMARA

I don't know.

ILYIN

Oh, you don't know! . . .

TAMARA

I wouldn't think less of you . . . Only, you know, a man should, after all, do the biggest thing he's capable of.

ILYIN

Who's capable of what, that's quite a problem! . . . Let's go, shall we?

TAMARA

Where?

ILYIN

With me.

TAMARA

(*laughs*) Just suddenly? Out of the blue? You must think!

ILYIN

Without thinking! What about it?

TAMARA

(*laughs*) All right, let's go . . . But what am I going to do there? I'll have to work, after all.

ILYIN

There are jobs everywhere.

TAMARA

What about Slava? He'll be lost here, he'll tie himself up in knots.

ILYIN

All right, he'll tie himself up in knots and he'll untie the knots.

58

TAMARA

Why are you teasing me? What would happen if I were to agree and to come. After all, you don't know me! (*Throwing out her arms, she spins round, then sits*)

ILYIN

Well? . . . What's it to be, Toma?

TAMARA

Do you really mean this? . . . What's the matter with you? You're so restless. Why? There was plenty to worry about before. But why now? Now we'll decide everything calmly. There's no great hurry now.

ILYIN

That's that. It's quite clear.

TAMARA

No, it isn't clear. I want to know what's happened.

ILYIN

I told you.

TAMARA

And I don't believe you. You can't think like that. Anyone else, yes, but not you.

ILYIN

I'm afraid that's how I am. It's time you accepted it.

TAMARA

No! You've a low opinion of yourself. You were always afraid of difficulties, never believed in yourself — that's true. But now you've achieved what you wanted and I respect you for it. Yet, there you go, the same thing all over again! You drop the work you love. You sacrifice your vocation. And what's it for! . . . If it is all a joke, then forgive me, I don't understand. Perhaps I have no sense of humor.

ILYIN

And supposing I simply wanted to find out how you felt about

me? Would you follow me to the end of the world or wouldn't
you? What would you say in that case?

TAMARA

I'll tell you. If you really are dishonest – or empty – go where
you like, but alone. I'm not going to run after you like a little
bitch. Do you understand?

ILYIN

Of course.

TAMARA

Are you offended?

ILYIN

(*rising*) All right, it's time to pack. You might buy me something to eat on the journey. I'm not giving up my comforts,
while you're making up your mind about my morals.

TAMARA

All right. (*She stops by the door*) Sasha, what's the matter
with you?

ILYIN

With me? Nothing.

TAMARA

Sasha, my dear, tell me. I'll understand.

ILYIN

Run along, run along . . . (*He goes into the other room.
Tamara stands by the door, sighs and goes out. When Ilyin
returns with his bag, the room is empty. He checks the con-
tents of the bag and closes it.*) Slava! (*Slava enters*) I want to
talk to you. Don't do anything to offend Toma. Don't drink
vodka. It blunts one's memory. Well, all the best.

SLAVA

Why, are you leaving already? Now?

ILYIN

(*quickly*) Business, my friend, business. One must go and labor.

SLAVA

Still, it's a pity. I suppose I've got used to you, more or less. Aleksandr Petrovich, I'm up for the grant tomorrow. You couldn't stick around another day, could you?

ILYIN

Another time. Yes, I keep forgetting to ask, why did you hit on chemistry of all things?

SLAVA

It was Aunt Toma who insisted. She has an *idée fixe* about it.

ILYIN

Consider yourself lucky. Chemistry, my dear brother, is the most abstract, most logical, and at the same time most practical of the sciences. But for someone who couldn't care less, chemistry spells ruin. Hell, you must adore the smell of ammonia, the smell of hydrogen sulphide. The true chemist arrives in the lab in his best suit. When he handles them, alkali don't splash and acids don't burn . . . Come on, show me your hand. Is that a chemist's hand? A chemist, with his bare hands, will lift any container off any burner. Got that?

SLAVA

Got that.

ILYIN

Then what are your conclusions about your future?

SLAVA

Quite so. I'm going to advance science backwards, and forwards. Still, it's a pity you're leaving today. You could have gone to the institute this evening to have a look round the old walls. There is a discussion tomorrow: "Can one assume that the unsuccessful student is honest?" followed by a review of studies. We've got some pretty wise guys.

ILYIN

I can't, old man.

SLAVA

To be honest, I promised the boys to introduce them to you. And you wouldn't find it without interest. We've got some original types. Igor, for instance — there's a personality. First of all, he's clever. Though some consider that he only appears to be clever because of his glasses. Incidentally he writes curious verse. I've persuaded him to read you some. I wonder what you'll say. Aleksandr Petrovich, now tell me frankly — do you think me over-familiar and talkative?

ILYIN

Don't spend your time in self-analysis. I like you.

SLAVA

(*very anxiously*) Personally, I hate people who can't leave you alone. On the other hand, we're sufficiently adult to talk openly. Yes, you appeal to me too. There it is. Our conversation has grown rather childish. Funny! Tell me, what do you intend to do during your leave? How about snatching a fortnight's boating on the Volga? What's your attitude to a venture of that kind?

ILYIN

My attitude is positive.

SLAVA

Perhaps, we could settle the details by post, shall we? Only do leave your address.

ILYIN

All right, there's time for that. Now as to theory. Once you make a mistake about a woman, it's bad. She'll ruin your existence for the rest of your life. But it's a hundred times worse, if out of stupidity, you by-pass a worthwhile person. I'm talking of Katya. Has that sunk in? Don't say anything. What's the pressure there?

SLAVA

(*looking at the clock*) Nine.

62

ILYIN

It's time. (*He takes Tamara's scarf off the hook and slips it into his pocket*)

SLAVA

That belongs to Aunt Toma.

ILYIN

It doesn't matter. (*He puts on his coat*)

SLAVA

(*understanding something*) Aren't you going to wait for her?

ILYIN

She's already downstairs, in the front hall. Well, all the best. Good-bye, old man.

SLAVA

But she'll go psychotic, if you leave like this, without saying good-bye. You know what she's like.

ILYIN

Don't let's argue. I'm in a hurry.

SLAVA

(*standing in front of the door*) Aleksandr Petrovich, you aren't telling the truth. What's the matter? Open up, I'll be as silent as the grave.

ILYIN

Listen, stop playing the fool, I've a train to catch. (*Half in fun, half in earnest, they fight by the door*) Have you gone crackers, or what?

SLAVA

Toma hasn't scared you, surely? Are you afraid she won't let you go? Don't be afraid, she won't say a word, on my head be it. Only you must wait for her.

ILYIN

An ultimatum, is it?

(*A short tussle. Ilyin throws Slava aside. Slava leaps up immediately and again seizes hold of Ilyin.*)

SLAVA

She's never had anyone except you! In such circumstances, the least one can do is to take one's leave! . . .

(*Ilyin carries Slava out into the hall. Then Slava is hurled into the room and falls flat on the floor. He picks himself up, shrugs, and gives a wry laugh. He sits on the writing desk and starts whistling thoughtfully. Tamara enters.*)

TAMARA

Our door is open.

SLAVA

Close it.

TAMARA

And where's Aleksandr Petrovich?

SLAVA

He said you were waiting downstairs. Didn't you see him off?

TAMARA

(*stands in silence, her shopping bag in her hand, then goes to the table, and automatically places the shopping on the table*) Yes, I did. (*She goes to the door*)

SLAVA

Aunt Toma! (*Tamara stops*) Don't humiliate yourself. Don't run after him.

(*Tamara slowly, methodically, tidies the room up. She takes a packet of cigarettes from the bookshelf and lights one. She plugs in the reflector, sits down on the stool, and without taking her coat off starts putting her hair in curlers. Slow blackout.*)

INTERVAL

SCENE 4

AUTHOR

> Hey you girls, from the old co-ed,
> My warmest greetings to you all,
> Forget the fact, however sad,
> You're thirty plus and in the fall.
>
> For you will still show off and shine,
> For you will still turn many a head.
> Despite evacuation, occupation,
> Your beauty's still alive, not dead.

And so the fourth evening.
(*A coat rack and a small chest of the kind found in a hall are on the stage. The telephone rings. A jacket flung over his shoulders, Ilyin enters and picks up the receiver.*)

ILYIN

Yes . . . Leningrad. Timofeyev? Just a moment. Misha, for
you . . . Hey, you're wanted on the phone!

(*Timofeyev enters, a gloomy man in pajamas, with ruffled
hair. He's about to take the receiver when there's a ring at the
door.*)

TIMOFEYEV

Who's that?

TAMARA'S VOICE

Excuse me, does Mikhail Timofeyev live here?

TIMOFEYEV

Yes.

(*Ilyin in a panic shakes his head and waves his arms, drop-
ping the receiver in its place. As he goes out, he whispers:* "I'm
not here." *Timofeyev opens the door. Tamara enters.*)

TAMARA

I'm sorry I'm so late . . . But sometimes it can't be helped
. . . I wanted to ask you for news of Ilyin, Aleksandr Petrovich.

TIMOFEYEV

(*vaguely*) Aleksandr Petrovich?

TAMARA

(*very politely*) You were students together at the institute.

TIMOFEYEV

Oh, Sasha! Yes, he was at the institute. Why, do you need him
right now? Immediately?

TAMARA

No, of course not! I only wanted to inquire after him. I'm
sorry it's so late.

TIMOFEYEV

(*looks at his watch, holds it to his ear, shakes it*) I had my
watch mended yesterday, today it's stopped.

TAMARA

It often happens. They mend it . . .

TIMOFEYEV

What?

TAMARA

I was saying, they mend the watch, but they don't mind if it goes or not.

TIMOFEYEV

(*with a shiver*) The heating's off, damn them. Won't you sit down. I'll go and put some more clothes on. (*He disappears. Tamara sits on the chest. She sits there stiff with embarrassment. Quiet music from the loudspeaker. Timofeyev, wrapped up, enters once again and speaks drily.*) Well, what can I do for you?

TAMARA

I wanted to inquire about Ilyin. Do you know where he is?

TIMOFEYEV

(*quickly*) Well, he did come round and look me up.

TAMARA

When?

TIMOFEYEV

I didn't make a note of the date, perhaps ten days ago . . .

TAMARA

Did he say he'd come and see you again?

TIMOFEYEV

No, he didn't.

TAMARA

Did he leave his address?

TIMOFEYEV

He didn't leave his address either.

TAMARA

Hmmm . . . What you'd call friends. So you met him and

67

didn't ask him anything . . . (*She goes to the front door, but stops and turns*)

TIMOFEYEV

Well, I asked him how things were and he asked me how things were . .

TAMARA

(*coming back*) Well, and how were things?

TIMOFEYEV

You see, I've come on business and I'm staying with relatives. So you find me here by accident. (*The telephone rings*) Yes! . . . Timofeyev speaking. Podgorsk? Hullo! I haven't got Podgorsk? No one's putting the receiver down! . . . I'll hang on, yes, yes . . .

TAMARA

Does that mean that you're also working at the combine there?

TIMOFEYEV

(*holding the receiver*) Yes, I am. And who else?

TAMARA

Why, Ilyin, of course!

TIMOFEYEV

Oh, Ilyin! Why yes, that's possible.

TAMARA

What do you mean — possible? Don't you know! What's your job?

TIMOFEYEV

My job? Chief engineer.

TAMARA

(*suspiciously*) That's odd. Very odd. And Ilyin?

TIMOFEYEV

What about Ilyin?

TAMARA

He is at Podgorsk too, isn't he?

68

TIMOFEYEV

No, Ilyin — I don't know where he works.

TAMARA

(*understanding something*) I see.

TIMOFEYEV

(*into the receiver*) Yes, Timofeyev speaking . . . All right, I can hear you clearly, go on . . . I see . . . All in order . . . We've come to an agreement . . . Already! . . . Deaf as a coot! I'll be back on the twentieth, send the car to meet me . . . That's all. So long. (*He hangs up*) Actually, what are you to him, his wife?

TAMARA

Me? No, just a friend.

TIMOFEYEV

I sympathize.

TAMARA

Why do you sympathize?

TIMOFEYEV

All right, this isn't the time. Some other time, at leisure.

TAMARA

All the same, I'm interested. You started it. Please finish what you were saying.

TIMOFEYEV

I haven't started anything. I don't like interfering in other people's business.

TAMARA

Are you suggesting, perhaps, that he leads a muddled sort of life?

TIMOFEYEV

What a strange woman you are. I'm not suggesting anything.

TAMARA

Or are you suggesting that he's unbalanced, quick-tempered, that he was even sent down from the institute and so he isn't really to blame! The dean, whom Sasha was rude to, is disliked by all the present students as well . . . Well, all right, Sasha may have been in the wrong at the time . . . But he was right when he said: "What counts is not to be in the right, but to correct one's mistakes in time."

TIMOFEYEV

And didn't he?

TAMARA

Well, the war started, you know! . . .

TIMOFEYEV

(*Ilyin can also hear*) I joined up too. But after the war I ate my porridge without any fat, at night I used to load cabbages in the harbor and sat through the lectures in a wooden stupor. What did he do?

TAMARA

What did he do?

TIMOFEYEV

He didn't stay the course at the institute. Why spend another three years at it? He remembered he was good at sport, won some medal or other, left a few superfluous teeth in the ring, and cooled down. Then he volunteered to go north somewhere . . .

TAMARA

North? . . .

TIMOFEYEV

I still don't know exactly what he does there . . .

TAMARA

But you envy him.

TIMOFEYEV

Me!?

TAMARA

He won a medal, but not you. He went north, but not you. Wherever he goes, they like him. He gets away with everything. He has talent! Even at school they had a nickname for him: gum arabic chemist — that's how clever he was at chemistry. And at the institute it wasn't you who helped him with his work, but he helped you!

TIMOFEYEV

(*with a laugh*) What a memory!

TAMARA

He didn't boast about it, it just came out . . . I understand now why he left me. Without any explanation. But it hurts all the same. He didn't think about me at all. And now I'm running after him. You'll say that I'm humiliating myself. Maybe. But I'm thinking of him, you know, not myself! But probably that isn't how it seems to everyone else.

TIMOFEYEV

Now, please calm down, you mustn't go on like this . . .

TAMARA

You know, I really live alone. It's all right during the week. My work's interesting, responsible, I have the feeling, always, that people need me. But on the days off — it's not too good. I don't want to go anywhere. There are couples, couples everywhere, while I am alone. Once in the tram I thought: "If only I could go on and on and never get there." Can you imagine? And at home, I feel so awful, suddenly, because the floor's polished and everything is in its place . . . Throwing things all over the room makes it still worse, tidying it all up again . . . (*She buttons her coat*)

TIMOFEYEV

Your neck's bare, you'll catch cold.

TAMARA

It's all right. I've lost my scarf somewhere. (*Timofeyev takes a scarf from the coat rack and throws it round her neck*) What are you doing? What's that for?

71

TIMOFEYEV

A keepsake.

TAMARA

(*returning it to him*) No, don't.

TIMOFEYEV

Wait, I'll see you home.

TAMARA

No, don't.

TIMOFEYEV

Do leave your address, at any rate. I'll come round if I hear anything.

TAMARA

The address is easy: Vostaniye Twenty-Two, flat two. Will you remember? Good-bye.

(*Tamara goes. Timofeyev sits on the chest gloomily, and lights a cigarette. Ilyin enters and looks at Timofeyev in silence.*)

ILYIN

Yes, it's an amusing situation . . .

TIMOFEYEV

Couldn't be more amusing.

ILYIN

I remember when I was wounded — there I was shivering in the ambulance, pressed to the side, with a splinter in the lung. I felt if I bent down at all, I'd have blood gushing out of my mouth. I thought to myself — you won't live long, you've had it. And I only had one thought in my head: "If only I were allowed to live another year. An enormous year. A million of such unending minutes. What wouldn't I do in that year!" I'd work in some lab for sixteen, twenty hours a day. The devil only knows, I might have been capable of doing something worthwhile! . . . (*He wrinkles up his face, shakes his head*) That was a fine description you gave of me. You really are

72

a swine. (*Timofeyev does not answer*) And in the name of all that's holy, will you please explain why you gave her your autobiography? What business is it of hers if you're chief engineer or not? And in Podgorsk, too! Why does she need your address? Why didn't you tell her your salary, while you were about it, and how many women friends you've had? What did I ask you? Tell her there's no one here, don't know anything. It was quite simple. But no, you had to bibble-babble, gibble-gabble. Windbag!

TIMOFEYEV

I've never lied to anyone in my life. I don't know how and you aren't going to force me to do it again!

ILYIN

Don't shout, you'll wake the old people.

TIMOFEYEV

Here's my advice to you. Run after her and grovel at her feet.

ILYIN

Out of the question.

TIMOFEYEV

Why?

ILYIN

You see, there are women with dimples in their cheeks and there are women without. Tamara's the only woman in the world with a dimple on one cheek.

TIMOFEYEV

Stop clowning.

ILYIN

Do you realize, I lied to her. I'm chief engineer, I blurted out. Well, you know, I used to be a sort of Mendeleyev in her mind's eye. Not worth disappointing her, I thought. Then I saw that things were more serious than I'd expected. Sooner or later I had to lay my cards on the table. What was I to do? Confess? What about the disgrace? Let her think I'm the desperate, thoughtless, well, the unpractical type. Better that way. Women can forgive that. I'm fed up with all this, I said, let's go to the devil somewhere north . . . Now, if she'd agreed — I'd have taken her with me and then it would have sorted itself out somehow. But no, she had to work it out first, reason it out, penetrate into all the circumstances of my life. But I don't want her penetration! I have the right to live as I like and not to have to answer to anyone. And that goes for you too. Prosecutor! I spat at her woman's heart with the very best of intentions. There's pride for you! And I'm fed up with you, rather. I'm going.

TIMOFEYEV

Where are you going in the middle of the night!

ILYIN

I'll manage. (*He puts on his coat and goes*)

(*Blackout.*)

SCENE 5

AUTHOR

The fifth evening.

Have you noticed how much sunlight an icicle holds? It lets fall bright drops, one after the other, and still it glitters! No, it is not spring yet, far from it. And this session is not over either.

(*Tamara's room. Slava is working. Katya is playing the guitar in a corner.*)

KATYA

Is it true that nobody weighs anything on the moon?

SLAVA

The moon does have gravity, but six times less.

KATYA

Really, I was told that . . .

SLAVA

Weightlessness sets in at the point where the gravity of the earth is balanced by the gravity of the moon.

KATYA

In the atmosphere?

SLAVA

There's no atmosphere there. It's space without air.

KATYA

Really, I was told that . . . Slava!

SLAVA

What?

KATYA

Didn't he return?

SLAVA

Haroun-al-Raschid fled faster than the fallow deer, faster than the hare before the eagle.

KATYA

Where to?

SLAVA

The direction is not known. Can't we talk about something else?

KATYA

Please do. Have you read what the paper says about you today?

SLAVA

Who do you mean by "you"?

KATYA

The chemical industry. The enormous prospects.

SLAVA

Don't worry about the prospects. Chemistry is the science of the future. The most abstract of the sciences and at the same time the most practical.

KATYA

When's the thermodynamics paper?

76

SLAVA

(*wrinkling up his face*) Why must you always be so beastly! I still have notes to copy. As for time!

KATYA

Ask Lidochka.

SLAVA

I have.

KATYA

Doesn't the copy cat work? (*Pause. Slava shakes himself free of unpleasant forebodings and goes up to Katya. She moves aside.*) Hands!

SLAVA

Go to hell!

KATYA

Did you think I'd be easier than your girl students? Well, I'm not. You have to be disillusioned. (*Slava returns to the table*) You probably think that my work is easy. You're wrong. It depends upon how you do it. You know, the subscribers actually like me very much. But the main thing is it's work with great prospects. I can rise to traffic supervisor. I don't know but I'm sorry you underestimate my expertise.

(*Tamara enters*)

TAMARA

Has anyone called?

SLAVA

No, he hasn't and he won't.

TAMARA

You see, Aleksandr Petrovich is still in town and I badly need to see him on business.

SLAVA

What business? Why do you need him? I'll lock you up in your room. You're mad. Take a look at yourself!

77

TAMARA

(*sadly*) What has he done to you, you're so angry with him?

SLAVA

Angry? Ha-ha! I despise him, that's all.

(*Tamara goes behind the screen and lies down on the bed*)

KATYA

(*going up to the screen*) By the way I know an address, where one could inquire about him.

SLAVA

You're out of this. (*beckoning her to him*) How do you know?

(*Tamara raises herself on the bed*)

KATYA

He was on the phone. I heard him.

SLAVA

Aren't you aware that telephone conversations are private?

KATYA

I don't want to hear but I can't help it. I don't like it. He phoned the Gastronome, corner of Liteyny and Pestel. Why don't you tell her, she could go round.

SLAVA

You make yourself out to be some heavenly creature, but let others go running about, humiliating themselves!

KATYA

And she should ask for Zoya from the grocery department. At least she'll find something out from her, one way or the other . . .

(*Slava begins working again*)

TAMARA

Will you have some tea?

KATYA

(*sitting down at the table*) With pleasure.

78

SLAVA

It's time for Katya to go home.

(*Katya looks at Slava, jumps up, snatches up her coat, and runs out without putting it on*)

TAMARA

What's got into you?

SLAVA

She chatters too much. (*He goes into his own room*)

(*Tamara gets up quietly, gets dressed, and goes out. Slow blackout. Lights up on the office of the Gastronome. Zoya is sitting at the table, a white coat over her street coat. She is holding a stack of small sheets of paper with exam questions, which she shuffles like a pack of cards. She takes the top sheet and reads.*)

ZOYA

Waffles, characteristics, quality, consistency. (*pause for thought*) Waffles – slightly porous discs with a pitted surface. They should have their own characteristic smell. (*She clicks a ball over on the abacus. Fed up with herself, she shakes her head. Again she shuffles the papers and takes the top one.*) Strong dessert wines. The most characteristic of the strong dessert wines are the port wines Massandra and Livadia. (*She clicks another ball over*)

WOMAN'S VOICE

Zoya!

ZOYA

What do you want?

WOMAN'S VOICE

Visitors for you. Are you in or out – what shall I say?

ZOYA

Who is it?

WOMAN'S VOICE

Friends, they say.

ZOYA

Let them in. (*Ilyin enters. His collar is turned up — it is cold outside. He puts down his suitcase, weighs himself on the weighing machine, and shakes his head.*) What a surprise! Well, now, did your friend make you welcome? Was she nice to you? (*Ilyin sits down*) What's all this melancholy? You must be an optimist these days. Take everything that life has to offer!

ILYIN

I have. There's nothing left.

ZOYA

Has madam thrown you out?

ILYIN

She has.

ZOYA

Well, tell me about your parting. I love it when they tell me about their partings! (*Ilyin says nothing, whistles a little*) A man in the prime of life. Shame on you. You have everything ahead of you.

ILYIN

I have everything ahead of me. When I was seventeen I had everything ahead of me.

ZOYA

You're a fine one to complain. You've seen so much of life. As good as Maxim Gorky.

ILYIN

Maxim Gorky wrote thirty tomes.

ZOYA

So what, it isn't everyone who has talent. I'm no better off. Here am I learning away and what's the point? Some people when they're asked a question never stop. But I come right out with all I have to say and shut up. They say it isn't enough.

80

ILYIN

You don't know me, how I used to be, with the world at my feet. A damp squib.

ZOYA

Is she interesting at least?

ILYIN

Who?

ZOYA

Your madam. Do bear in mind that a woman who is uninteresting is just like a man who's stupid.

ILYIN

I've gone completely to pieces between the lot of you. It's time to go home. Home to work.

ZOYA

I wish you success. Work maketh man.

ILYIN

Yes, it's time. The faint breeze of memory is already blowing in our faces . . .

ZOYA

I have an idea. Let's kiss, shall we?

ILYIN

Another time.

ZOYA

You're scared. I was joking. Do you know why I am so frivolous? Apparently my great-grandfather was French. Now, I'll tell you honestly, I can't stand the song that goes – I respect her, I adore her, I gratify her . . .

ILYIN

If only you'd be quiet.

ZOYA

Why should I be quiet. I'm at home.

ILYIN

(*getting up*) Hey-ho!

ZOYA

Where are you off to?

ILYIN

I'm going.

ZOYA

For good?

ILYIN

For good.

ZOYA

Then why did you come?

ILYIN

To say good-bye. (*He waves his train ticket*)

ZOYA

Good-bye then . . . (*They shake hands. Ilyin goes. She shouts after him.*) To hell with you, go and don't bother to look back. Oh, you fool! Where are you off to, what are you after? . . . (*No reply from Ilyin. She listens. He has gone. She sits down and shuffles the exam questions.*) Right. Grapes. Well, standard grapes must be standard. Grapes are mostly packed in sieves. (*She clicks a ball over*) Right. Vitamins. In the year one thousand eight hundred and eighty, the scientist Lukin proved that there are vitamins. Vitamin E preserves the nervous system. (*Another ball. Tamara enters.*) To see me?

TAMARA

To see you, yes. On a personal matter.

ZOYA

Take a seat. Only make it short. I have an exam tomorrow to raise my qualifications. The questions! They ought to ask the Minister of Trade.

TAMARA

(*sits*) I have to find Aleksandr Petrovich.

ZOYA

I'm sorry, what Aleksandr Petrovich?

TAMARA

His surname is Ilyin.

ZOYA

Do you mean Sasha?

TAMARA

Sasha, yes.

ZOYA

(*realizing whom she's talking to*) So it's a falling star. You mean, you're looking for him.

TAMARA

I have business with him.

ZOYA

Right. You mean, he's run away.

TAMARA

I know he comes here.

ZOYA

You should have held on to him earlier. No good waving one's fists after a fight.

TAMARA

I have to see him. Not for long.

ZOYA

You mean, he plays you up too.

TAMARA

What strange things you say.

ZOYA

Listen, my friend, he's well and truly anchored here, the anchor won't drift.

TAMARA

I'm not interested. My business is personal.

ZOYA

Well, mine isn't public. (*They look at each other in silence*)

TAMARA

Will you tell him I want to see him?

ZOYA

And what are you to him?

TAMARA

Just a friend. An old friend.

ZOYA

Marvelous. Well, I'm the new friend and he tells me everything. So the old friend comes to ask me how he is and where.

TAMARA

No, he doesn't tell me everything. Perhaps he's ashamed.

ZOYA

Ah-ha! They're not ashamed when they're in love. Love is
shameless, do bear that in mind . . . No, you don't suit each
other at all! Anyhow, he'll start being unfaithful to you in a
month's time. You'll find it unbearable. But I'll forgive him.
(*gradually getting excited*) Why, he doesn't know himself
what he needs! He still has youthful memories of you, that's
what disturbs him! Is it my fault he first met you and not me?
I looked better than you, do believe me. (*She fishes about in
her bag*) Here, take a look, that's how I was.

TAMARA

(*poisonously*) Yes, you've changed a lot.

ZOYA

Still, I've a long way to go before I'm as old as you. Surely,
you've thought about your age.

TAMARA

(*lightly*) Well, they say I'm well preserved.

ZOYA

Don't believe them, they're exaggerating. (*with sympathy*)
You should get married, that's what it is. To a good man.
Why not go to India. They say that to every one woman there,
there's a man and a half. Even a half would do.

84

TAMARA

Then you won't forget and tell him?

ZOYA

Do you think he'll come running back? (*Tamara says nothing*) Well, there's life while there's hope.

TAMARA

Good-bye.

ZOYA

The trouble is I shan't have the chance of telling him. You haven't got him — and I haven't got him.

TAMARA

How do you mean. Haven't you?

ZOYA

Just that. Go on looking for him. If you find him, give him my greetings. (*Tamara goes*) Right. Starch. (*remembering*) Starch — it's minute particles, which are invisible to the simple, aided eye. (*She looks into her notebook*) Unaided eye! (*She bursts into tears*)

(*The forestage. Ilyin is sitting at a table in a railway restaurant. Katya enters with a metal disc in her hand.*)

KATYA

Comrade Ilyin!

ILYIN

Oh! . . .

KATYA

Let's get out of here.

ILYIN

Where have you come from, you lovely child?

KATYA

Me? From the exchange.

ILYIN

And how did you get here?

KATYA

Me? I was walking past and saw you standing by the front hall, where Tamara Vasilyevna lives.

ILYIN

I wasn't standing anywhere.

KATYA

Well, maybe you weren't. I just thought you were. You can eat the herring, but I'll take the vodka back. You haven't touched the carafe, so they have to take it back. (*Ilyin pours himself a glass and drinks*) Comrade Ilyin, you shouldn't! That's how it all starts. Haven't you seen the documentary film — "It Prevents Us from Living"? . . . Let's get out of here. A young woman can't go on sitting here. What will they think of me?

ILYIN

Never think of what they think. You must learn not to depend on other people's opinion.

KATYA

How can I? After all we don't live alone but among people, in a society . . . (*Ilyin pours himself another glass*) Aleksandr Petrovich, you shouldn't! Let's go and see Tamara Vasilyevna instead. She wants to see you about something.

ILYIN

Je ferai ce que je peux.

KATYA

What?

ILYIN

For your sake, I'll do what I can.

KATYA

Thank you.

ILYIN

Only not that.

KATYA

Why not! What a strange man you are . . . She loves you so much! It happens once in a lifetime and then not to everyone. Other people go on living without, thinking everything's all right. Somewhere I read that there's no such thing as love, only sympathy. It's not true! Is there anything to compare with love? Without it a person dries up.

ILYIN

In that case, let's drink to Tamara Vasilyevna!

KATYA

Oh, really! Then I'll drink too. I'll drink as much as you drink.

ILYIN

Good for you! (*He pours out a glass for her*)

KATYA

Except that I mustn't. I'll be drunk immediately.
(*They drink. Katya chokes and quickly eats something.*)

ILYIN

Yes, one's got to get used to the idea that the best has been left behind.

KATYA

(*having drunk, she begins to agree*) Well, yes, it's true. You know, I'm not all that young either. I'm nineteen and already my nerves have deteriorated.

ILYIN

You were talking about Tamara Vasilyevna.

KATYA

Me? I don't remember.

ILYIN

Ideally one can only live with a woman who sparks you off.

KATYA

I think Tamara Vasilyevna really does spark.

87

ILYIN

The war started — she was the only one to see me off. We were sitting in lorries with the women weeping all around, but she looked up and said: "You see, you're going to have such an unfeeling . . ." and then stopped. "What?" I asked. The engines were roaring, so I couldn't hear. "What did you say? I didn't understand." "I said: You see, you're going to have such an unfeeling wife." The lorries moved off. She ran behind. She ran in silence. Then the engine conked out or something — and we stopped. And she stopped. She leaned against the exhaust and stared. Off we went again; she started running behind. Then she couldn't keep up . . . (*He pours himself a drink*) You've had enough now.

KATYA

(*almost in tears*) If you are going to drink, I'll drink too! (*roaring with laughter*) One of our girls, who had long hair in plaits, cut it off, put on a tight blouse and a skirt with slits, and she had boy friends immediately. Tell me, why's that? The boys can be just as bad. As soon as one of them meets you he asks you where you live, in case it's a long way for him to see you home . . . Aleksandr Petrovich, when I saw him, it was as though a bell rang out in my chest!

ILYIN

Who did you see?

KATYA

Who? Slava!

ILYIN

Well, there you are. And what are you doing sitting here! Go to him. Since you know there are those two little words: "Too late." All right, . . . you will find out later! But do what I tell you anyway. It is those who are the failures who always give the best advice.

88

KATYA

But why are you a failure? You're a great man. The way you understand chemistry, Slava says it's unique!

ILYIN

Chemistry, my dear Katya, is nothing but a dream. Chemistry is the bluebird. But at the back of beyond, there's a hamlet called Ust-Omul. The frosts there are minus forty degrees centigrade and the mist on the ground is like milk. If you puff, there's a booming noise, like an engine whistle, and the air freezes. You can't move a car, it doesn't grip the ground. On the slopes the rubber comes off in strips. But you spend the day at the wheel, you know. If the trip is urgent, you don't sleep at night. You have a bite of something, sitting in your cabin, and press on. Or you get stuck in the taiga, five hundred kilometers from the nearest hamlet, and wait till they come and dig you out. That's what a driver's job is like.

KATYA

You mean, you've told a pack of lies, and you're a driver?

ILYIN

I'm now in charge of a garage. They've promised to start a transport center.

KATYA

But why did you lie?

ILYIN

Just out of petty vanity.

KATYA

You mean, you wanted to make yourself out superior?

ILYIN

Now, we've had our discussion — it's enough. Off you go, Katya.

KATYA

What about you?

ILYIN

I'll stay here.

KATYA

I'm not going alone.

ILYIN

(*fed up*) Oh! . . .

(*He knocks the glass over. So does Katya. He thumps it down on the table. So does Katya. They stare at each other with shining eyes. Blackout. Lights up on Tamara's room. We find the aunt and nephew arrested in mid-action, talking. She had been folding the tablecloth, he had just unrolled a large sheet of drawing paper.*)

TAMARA

They were sitting in the lorries, everyone weeping all around. And I said to him: "You see, you're going to have such an unfeeling wife" . . . Slava, don't be cross. It's all over!

SLAVA

If it's all over, why give way to your memories?

TAMARA

That's why I am giving way. I didn't give way before. The lorries moved off and I started running. I ran in silence. Then for some reason their lorry stopped. And I stopped and stared at him. They moved off again, and I started running again . . .

SLAVA

Just one thing I don't understand. It's only in novels that people fall in love without knowing why, but in life there's a reason for falling in love.

TAMARA

Slava, no, he isn't the type of man you think he is. Not at all like that, not at all!

SLAVA

I envy the people who like everyone.

TAMARA

It's a long time since I liked everyone.

SLAVA

That's progress.

TAMARA

Hardly. People have often thought that life's more bad than good. But, well, time passes, and what is there left? Lenin, Giordano, Bruno, Pushkin. They'll always be remembered! But the inquisitors, oppressors, tsars — they're nearly all forgotten. One still learns about individual leaders in history lessons, and even then one muddles up which tsar came after which.

SLAVA

You aren't without logic.

(*Suddenly silent, they continue as in a movie which starts up again the actions interrupted by their conversation*)

TAMARA

(*absentmindedly*) How are your trade union affairs getting on?

SLAVA

Not at all. Why should I start creating on everyone else's behalf! These elections — so called! Everyone had an alibi. One of them said that he sang in the choir. Another said that he lived out of town. A third said — you can't elect me, I stifle other people's initiative. Marvelous! And I just went out for a moment and, blow me down, they elected me!

TAMARA

You should be ashamed to talk like that! You are a trade union organizer! The students arrive from God knows where. Some live in private flats. You know best who needs putting up in a hostel, who needs assistance out of the director's fund. Some are embarrassed and would never apply on their own. Then there's culture-for-the-masses. Particularly for strangers to Leningrad. You should go with them to theatres, museums . . . arrange excursions on foot or by coach to famous places. The union has its funds for this kind of thing. Oh, what an egotist you are! . . . Tomorrow I'll bring you a form — a scale of members' contributions. You'll put it up on the board for all to see.

SLAVA

(*sighing*) All right.

TAMARA

I'm going to tidy up your room. (*She goes into the other room*)

SLAVA

Your room! How many of you are there? One!

(*The doorbell rings. Tamara returns.*)

TAMARA

It's him! (*She sinks down on a chair*)

SLAVA

Shall I open it?

TAMARA

No, wait. Someone else will. (*They sit in silence. Katya's voice can be heard.*) Your Katya's come.

(*Tamara again disappears into the other room. Katya enters. She's thoroughly ginned up.*)

KATYA

(*warning him the moment she opens the door*) It isn't you I've come to see. (*Approaching the table, she sulkily inspects his charts*) Still whinnying after your Lidochka? Own up, own up!

SLAVA

Breathe out! (*She breathes out*) Where did you get so stinko?

KATYA

What's it got to do with you? (*She stretches out her arm and points at her handkerchief, which she has dropped deliber-*

92

ately) Pick it up! (*Slava picks it up*) A chair! (*Slava brings her a chair*) Not here, over there! (*Slava places the chair against the wall. Katya sings to herself as she dances round the room.*) Oh, what am I singing! We must have the czardas! (*She dances the czardas in front of Slava*) How long must I go on dancing! It's your turn now!

SLAVA

You balmy?

KATYA

You must do whatever a woman asks you to. Otherwise I shall leave. Hold your hands out! In, out, in, out! Got that? (*Tamara enters*)

TAMARA

What's going on?

KATYA

(*to Tamara*) He is gifted, but he must be more systematic in his studies. (*to Slava*) Glass of water! (*Slava gives her a glass of water*) Drink it! . . .

SLAVA

(*putting down the glass*) Well, you know . . .

KATYA

Tamara Vasilyevna, I have to discuss a most important matter with you. May I lie down?

TAMARA

Come and lie down on my bed. I'll get something to tuck round you.

KATYA

(*to Slava*) Something to tuck round me. Do you hear? (*Slava brings a rug. Katya lies down and he tucks her up.*) Now get the notebook out of my coat. The pocket. (*Slava takes out a fat notebook*) It's for you!

SLAVA

(*opening the notebook*) What is it?

KATYA

I've been tidying up after Lidochka and I discovered her famous lecture notes on thermodynamics. I copied them for you.

SLAVA

What, for the whole year?

KATYA

I had nothing to do . . .

SLAVA

But how much time did this hack-work take you?

KATYA

I sat up one night. Anyway, I had insomnia. Why do you call it hack-work? Don't you need it? It is for the session.

SLAVA

(*thoughtfully, to the tune of "C'est si bon"*) Se-ssi-on! Ta-ra-boom, ta-ra-boom . . . Thanks.

KATYA

Why are you standing there? Go and do some work! (*Slava, leafing through the notebook, goes into the other room*) Now what was it that I wanted to say? . . . Tamara Vasilyevna, I know what it was — Aleksandr Petrovich is no match for you. And he himself knows this perfectly well. Somewhere I have read the dictum — "On a man's grave you should inscribe not what he has been but what he might have been."

TAMARA

What grave? What's happened to him?

KATYA

Nothing's happened — it's a quotation. First of all, he's a liar. Apparently, he works at a transport center somewhere in the Arctic Circle. At a temperature of minus forty degrees centigrade. And in that awful cold he has to travel over the taiga.

TAMARA

(*shaking her by the shoulder*) Where did you see him? Is he still here? Where is he now?

94

KATYA

> I don't know. He brought me here and then went away some-
> where. Tamara Vasilyevna, you've shaken me up. I feel like
> an egg, when the white is all mixed up with the yolk. I am now
> goggle-moggle. Do you mind if I go to sleep?
>
> (*Doorbell. Tamara rushes off to open the door, then returns
> to the mirror and hastily tidies her hair. Knock on the door.*)

TAMARA

> Yes.
>
> (*Timofeyev enters*)

TIMOFEYEV

> How are you? Am I in the way?

TAMARA

> Of course not. Take your coat off.

TIMOFEYEV

> Not worth it. I only looked in for a moment. (*But he takes his
> coat off*)

TAMARA

> Do sit down.

TIMOFEYEV

> I haven't the time. (*But he sits down*) I saw the light in the
> window, so I decided to look in and see how things were. So
> this is where you live? Who lives there?

TAMARA

> My nephew.

TIMOFEYEV

> And what's that? (*He plugs in the reflector, which flares and
> goes out*)

TAMARA

> It's a reflector. You've fused it.

TIMOFEYEV

> (*examining the reflector*) Never mind, I'll take it away and
> mend it.

TAMARA

It's all right, my nephew will mend it. Slava!

(*Slava enters with the open notebook*)

SLAVA

Is Katya asleep? Aunt Toma, do you realize what she's done. She handed over to me all the lectures on thermodynamics for the whole session. The formulas as well. It's a hell of a job! An act of heroism, you know. For this one could nominate her for an award.

TAMARA

Stop chattering. You'll wake her up.

SLAVA

And the important thing is, she hasn't left anything out. It really looks as though she's gifted that way, don't you think? Perhaps she's a natural. It's rare with her looks, wouldn't you say? Actually, her appearance is very striking. Have you noticed?

TAMARA

All right, off you go, get on with your work. You've got your notes, don't waste your time.

SLAVA

Give me a shout when she wakes. (*He goes*)

(*Tamara goes up to the sleeping Katya and adjusts the rug. Katya wakes up.*)

KATYA

Where's Slava?

TAMARA

In the other room.

KATYA

I think I've offended him. Do you remember what I said to him?

TAMARA

No, I don't.

96

KATYA

Perhaps I should go and apologize. (*She puts her shoes on, goes to the door of the other room, and pauses*) Tamara Vasilyevna, what month was he born in?

TAMARA

In March.

KATYA

I'm four months older than he is. It's bad, isn't it?

TAMARA

Rubbish!

KATYA

Do you really think so? . . . (*She goes to Slava*)

TIMOFEYEV

(*taking the reflector to pieces at the table*) You wouldn't have a pair of pliers, would you?

TAMARA

(*absentmindedly*) Yes, I have.

TIMOFEYEV

And perhaps a screwdriver?

TAMARA

(*as before*) Yes.

TIMOFEYEV

Won't you give them to me?

TAMARA

(*without moving*) Yes . . . You came to tell me something, didn't you?

TIMOFEYEV

Well, actually, out of interest. Has Ilyin been to see you?

TAMARA

Aleksandr Petrovich? Why should he!

TIMOFEYEV

Don't you know where he is?

97

TAMARA

I have more important things to worry about. So much to do — all I need is time to get on. Do you know what it's like at the district office? There are girls straight from school. There are some who can't cope in any job. One girl's too quiet, another's too cocky. She turns up on duty straight from the skating rink. The mess she made! I told her — I'll throw your skates away and dock your pay. (*Doorbell. Tamara goes out, opens the door and returns, followed by Ilyin. She speaks simply.*) Haven't you left?

ILYIN

Tomorrow.

TAMARA

If you want to spend the night, the room's vacant.

ILYIN

(*to Timofeyev*) Oh! All the familiar faces!

TIMOFEYEV

(*mending the reflector*) Hullo!

ILYIN

(*to Tamara*) Don't believe anything he says. He's a married man with three children. What will he do with them?

TIMOFEYEV

You really are a clown. (*He gets up*)

ILYIN

Don't get up. (*All three sit down. Ilyin sits at the table in his coat, Tamara on the windowsill, Timofeyev with the reflector by the door.*) This is what I've come to say. Unless I'm mistaken, you've got it into your head that I'm a failure, in a manner of speaking. (*Katya and Slava enter, stand still, and listen*) Personally, I'm afraid I don't think so. I consider myself a useful member of society. And incidentally more useful than the lot of you put together. Just you try driving a Studebaker through the taiga. There you are behind the wheel

98

with all the elements against you. And supposing you have a hundred lads like this one under you? Not counting the porters, of whom there's a shortage, or the maintenance men, whom we don't get at all. It's one of two things: either they worship you or tie you up in knots and after a month send you to the mainland for a rest cure. It may seem strange, but I like it. So do realize, friends, that I don't intend to make myself out better than I am just to please you. A man must always be himself. That's the most profitable attitude to take. Yes, once in a while there comes a time when one's drawn to one's old childhood haunts and friends. It hasn't worked, has it? All the better. Do remember that I'm a free, gay, and happy man. And I shall yet find new forms of happiness. Which is what I wish you too. So on that note I'll say good-bye. (*He gets up*)

TAMARA

Sasha, I have a great respect for you.

ILYIN

Aha, so you have a great respect for me. You are proud of me.

TAMARA

Yes, I am proud.

ILYIN

Just so! Why are you frowning, chief engineer? Do I shock you?

TIMOFEYEV

It's all right. Only, you know, in situations like this, I do try not to work off my temper on others. Especially women. Let's go.

ILYIN

I'll go when my hostess tells me to go. (*to Tamara*) Should I go, perhaps?

TIMOFEYEV

> (*after looking at them carefully*) Oh, all right, I can see that
> you'll sort this out between you. (*He goes*)
> (*Ilyin stands there motionless. Then he quickly goes up to
> Tamara. He looks at her from under his brows, stops, then
> sits down with his back to her. Katya and Slava go back to
> their room, sit down on the divan side by side, quiet with
> concentration. Ilyin, without raising his eyes, turns toward
> Tamara and hides his face in her lap. Tamara does not move.*)

TAMARA

> I knew you'd come. I knew it!

ILYIN

> How has it happened? You're the best of them all and yet you
> fell in love with me. The eighth wonder of the world.

TAMARA

> The eighth? What are the others?

ILYIN

> I don't know.

TAMARA

> So honest. So wise. So good! . . . Do you remember you
> suggested going somewhere. Well, then, I'll come if you
> haven't changed your mind. Oh, why are you kissing my
> hands, they're dirty . . . Oh, why are you kissing my
> blouse! . . .

ILYIN

> It's all right, you won't regret it.

TAMARA

> I shan't regret it, Sasha, I shan't regret it!

ILYIN

> It's all right, you'll see.

TAMARA

> Yes, I'll see, Sasha, I'll see!

100

ILYIN

Toma! What haven't you had to put up with because of me!

TAMARA

No, you mustn't, don't think about me. I was all right here.
I've had a lot of happiness in my life. God grant it to all. And
then on the whole, I never get depressed. And then, everything will be different now, everything! . . . It's Sunday tomorrow. We could go on Lake Krasavitza. It's lovely there.
So they say — I haven't been yet. And it's very beautiful in
Pavlovsk . . . So they say — I haven't been there either.
(*both happy and afraid for her happiness*) Oh, if only we
don't have a war! . . .

FINAL BLACKOUT